The Flinders Ranges
South Australia

Text by Cil Dobré
Photography Pete Dobré

National Library of Australia Cataloguing-in-Publication Data:
Dobré, Cil.
The Flinders Ranges, South Australia
ISBN 0 9577063 1 6
1. Natural History - South Australia - Flinders Ranges - Pictorial works.
2. Flinders Ranges (S. Aust.) - Pictorial works.
I. Dobré, Pete, 1958- . II. Title.
994.237

Published and distributed by Pete Dobré's Oz Scapes
P.O. Box 305, Happy Valley, South Australia, 5159, Australia
Email: ozscapes@cobweb.com.au Phone/Fax: +61 8 8381 5895
Website: www.petedobre.com.au

Front Cover: Wilpena Pound
Title Page: Settler's Hut, Wilpena Pound

Map of the Flinders Ranges

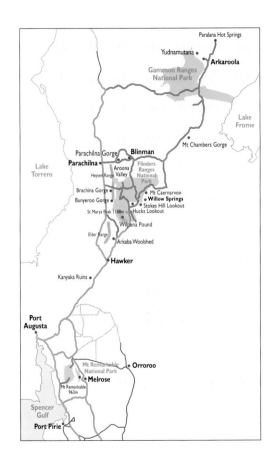

Paralana Hot Springs

Yudnamutana

Arkaroola

Gammon Ranges
National Park

Lake
Frome

Mt Chambers Gorge

Parachilna Gorge **Blinman**

Parachilna

Aroona
Valley

Flinders
Ranges
National
Park

Heysen Range

Lake
Torrens

Brachina Gorge

Mt Caernarvon

Bunyeroo Gorge

Willow Springs

St Marys Peak 1188m

Stokes Hill Lookout

Hucks Lookout

Wilpena Pound

Elder Range

Arkaba Woolshed

Hawker

Kanyaka Ruins

**Port
Augusta**

Mt Remarkable
National Park

Orroroo

Melrose

Mt Remarkable
963m

**Spencer
Gulf**

Port Pirie

The Flinders Ranges

The Flinders Ranges

One of South Australia's most popular tourist attractions lies in the inspiring region of the Flinders Ranges, with its spectacular scenery. North of Pt Pirie the ranges rise, curve northwards to Arkaroola, then descend into the desert country further north.

The first European to sight this rugged chain of mountains from the head of Spencer Gulf was Matthew Flinders in 1802, when circumnavigating Australia.

Old homestead ruins and ghost towns, railway tracks and stations, cemeteries and graves dot the region, accompanied by stories of hope, heartbreak and adventure from early settlers. Some came to graze the land, others to mine. Lacking knowledge of the land, isolation, drought, as well as misunderstanding and conflict with the Aboriginals eventually defeated many. However, small country towns still abound, like Melrose, Wilmington, Quorn, Hawker, Parachilna and Blinman, each supplying travellers' needs. Today the Flinders Ranges is mostly National Park, private property or leased pastoral land.

Historically a large Aboriginal population from several tribal groups lived in the Flinders Ranges, from whom names in this region, like Wilpena and Arkaroola originated.

When Sir Hans Heysen, the famous landscape artist, first visited the Flinders Ranges in the late 1920's, they provided him with amazing scope. He loved the twisted gums, the region's intense light and colours, the deep blue skies, the exposed rock faces with their variegated shades. His famous paintings achieved notoriety for the region.

Tourists now arrive to bush walk, camp, paint, bird-watch and photograph this diverse landscape of rugged mountain ranges, rolling hills, peaceful tree-lined gorges, creek beds of majestic red gums and broad sweeping plains.

As well, hundreds of fascinating walking trails, with magnificent vantage-point views, suit various interests and abilities. Short pleasant strolls lead along shady creek beds, while challenging climbs lead up mountain edges and through gorges to awe-inspiring vistas.

Visitors enjoy the Flinders Ranges' deep gorges, cut by wind and water, together with rock walls, sheer gullies and sharp peaks which glow intensely orange in the late afternoon sun. View reflections in the rock pools below.

Wilpena Pound with its natural amphitheatre, and only four and a half hours from Adelaide, remains a special feature in the central region of the Flinders Ranges. The gigantic crater-shaped bowl with its purple ridges, overhanging bluffs and jagged peaks is awesome.

The highest peak on the Pound's lip is St Marys Peak, 1190 metres which is visible for many kilometres. You may choose a 1-2 hour return stroll into the Pound, or a strenuous 4-6 hour return climb. From the top your reward will be a view down into the magnificent valleys and gorges, appreciating the shape of the Pound, together with the beauty of the surrounding rugged Australian landscape.

As you drive through the Flinders, whether Alligator Gorge or Mt Remarkable to the south, or the rugged ranges of the Gammons, or Arkaroola Wilderness Sanctuary to the north, delight in the land's range of colours: the blues, purples, reds and greens.

As you walk along creeks, where picturesque red gums glow, observe the intricate bark patterns, while enjoying the solitude. When rains bring flash floods, trickling creek beds may quickly become raging torrents. Please heed the strict rule of the Flinders and do not set up camp in a creek bed.

Whatever the weather conditions, enjoy the area's beauty. Rain, fog, mist, cloud and sunlight provide contrasts of light, colours, and shadows on the ranges. Return to favourite spots in varying seasons and weather extremes to appreciate the contrasts.

Whether you take a flight over the Pound and nearby valleys, or over the rugged ranges of Arkaroola Wilderness Sanctuary, appreciate an unforgettable experience.

See nature at its best with abundant birdlife. Flocks of Corellas, Galahs, Honeyeaters, Kites, Falcons and Parrots live in the bush. Wedge-tailed Eagles soar across the sky, looking for a carcass to devour. Emus stroll around while Kangaroos, Wallabies and Euros hop along. Keep watch for the Yellow-footed Rock Wallaby, as its fur glows in the sunlight.

If you enjoy wildlife, natural landscapes, wide open spaces, serenity and beauty, head for the Flinders Ranges. You will wonder and contemplate the beauty of creation.

Yudnamutana

Brachina Gorge

Bunyeroo Valley

Aroona Creek

Sturt Desert Pea

Stark Light

Heysen Range

Cazneaux Tree

Wedge-tailed Eagle

Evening Hue

Hucks Lookout

Parachilna Gorge

Western-grey Kangaroo

Emu

Yellow-footed Rock Wallaby

Evening Light on Settler's Hut

24

Settler's Hut

Approaching Storm on Wilpena Pound

Elder Range

Hayward Bluff

Hucks Lookout

Blinman

North Blinman Hotel

Main Street Blinman

Prairie Hotel - Parachilna

Old Ghan Restaurant and Gallery - Hawker

Wilpena Pound

Sunrise on Wilpena Pound

St Marys Peak

Hucks Lookout

Rawnsley Bluff

Skytrek – Willow Springs from Stokes Hill Lookout

Parachilna Gorge

Hucks Lookout

Arkaba Woolshed

Elder Range

Bunyeroo Valley

Western Pound Wall

Arkaroola - Northern Flinders Ranges

Bararranna Gorge - Arkaroola - Northern Flinders Ranges

Stubbs Waterhole - Arkaroola - Northern Flinders Ranges

Bararranna Gorge - Arkaroola - Northern Flinders Ranges

Drifting Sands

Kanyaka Ruins

Before the Rain

After the Rain

Eucalyptus Art Forms

Mt Chambers Gorge - Northern Flinders Ranges

Gammon Ranges National Park

Bunyip Chasm – Gammon Ranges National Park

Parachilna Gorge